The Antelope Valley Station to Neset Transmission Project

A Critical Review

Thomas D. Isern

White Paper No. 1

Center for Heritage Renewal
North Dakota State University

Fargo, February 2014

Preface

This white paper originated as a submission by the Center for Heritage Renewal to the Rural Utilities Service. As described herein, the center earlier had entered the regulatory process for the Antelope Valley to Neset Transmission Project, as proposed by Basin Electrical Power Cooperative. The center on September 4, 2013, gave a submission to the North Dakota Public Service Commission, pointing out that documents presented to the PSC by Basin had omitted mention of the historic site of the Battle of Killdeer Mountain, which lay squarely athwart Basin's proposed route for a 365kV power transmission line. Additional developments and disclosures moved the center to enter into the process once again, with an expanded submission to the Rural Utilities Service.

The authorized mission of the Center for Heritage Renewal is "to identify, preserve, and capitalize on the heritage resources of North Dakota and the northern plains." Adhering to this mission, and alarmed by the direct threat to the heritage resource of the Killdeer Mountain Battlefield, the center now publishes its RUS submission as White Paper No. 1. We have identified the heritage resource. We speak for its preservation, so that future generations will retain it as heritage capital.

The Antelope Valley Station to Neset Transmission Project
A Critical Review

Principal Author, Thomas D. Isern

Submission to Rural Utilities Service
Submitted February 3, 2014

Commenting on
*Antelope Valley Station to Neset Transmission Project,
Supplemental Draft Environmental Impact Statement*

A White Paper from the

Center for Heritage Renewal
North Dakota State University
heritagerenewal.org

Contents	
Prologue: Coals to Newcastle	2
Alternatives	5
Cover-Up	9
Diversions	17
Impacts	20
Conclusions	23
Appendices	26

Prologue: Coals to Newcastle

The current proposal by Basin Electric is to build a new, 278-mile (or more), 345kV transmission line, the Antelope Valley Station to Neset Transmission Project, across a project area comprising Mercer, Dunn, McKenzie, Williams, and Mountrail counties of North Dakota. The line is intended, says Basin, to serve the "long-term needs of northwestern North Dakota."

Citizens, organizations, and agencies have protested the plan by Basin Electric for various reasons, a chief one (and the one of concern in this submission) being that the proposed 345kV transmission line transects, and thereby degrades the historical integrity of, the Killdeer Mountain Battlefield. A submission to the North Dakota Public Service Commission by the Center for Heritage Renewal (see Appendix 1) argued that the Killdeer Mountain Battlefield is the "most significant historic site in North Dakota" and, more poetically, "The Gettysburg of the Plains." These assessments of significance by the center stand publicly unquestioned.

The center further argued that construction of Basin's 345kV transmission line would degrade the historical integrity of the battlefield to an unacceptable degree. The most recent (December 2013) draft environmental impact statement before the Rural Utilities Service argues to the contrary. That disagreement will be dealt with later in this submission.

It is easy, however, to lose sight of larger and fundamental considerations when disputing specific matters on the ground. We might easily be diverted into spending large amounts of time and ink on matters of degree and distinctions of terminology—certainly this is the rhetorical strategy employed in the cultural resources section of the DEIS here referenced. Before moving on to the question of how much degradation of integrity is acceptable, should we not first consider whether there need be any degradation at all? The Center for Heritage Renewal, in line with its expertise, offers a historical perspective on that question.

The Basin Electric website provides an organizational history that is both informative and too modest. Basin originated in 1960 when a consortium of regional power companies formed an entity they called the Giant Power Cooperative. Giant had intentions of building power plants and supplying regional cooperatives that had sprung up with the assistance of the Rural Electrification Administration. Organizers soon realized that cooperative organization would be as advantageous for them as for the cooperatives they hoped to supply. So in 1961 they transformed their enterprise into Basin Electric Power Cooperative. This enabled them to obtain a construction loan from the REA. Thus from the beginning, Basin Electric has prospered through public entrepreneurship, turning federal funding to regional advantage. Basin's first power plant, Leland Olds, came on line in 1966. Then and now, Basin has taken advantage of the natural resources of west-central North Dakota: lignite from the Knife River valley, and water from the Missouri River.

We say that Basin is too modest because its online history does not convey the monumental importance of its enterprise to North Dakota. Basin built and expanded during the era of consolidation on the northern plains, when North Dakota suffered near-catastrophic decline, economically and demographically. When agriculture was in crisis, and industry was failing to root, Basin Electric was life support for the regional economy. As North Dakotans, we owe Basin a great, historic debt of thanks.

Organizations evolve and sometimes change in character, and leadership must stay abreast of change. In January 2014 the Basin board of directors accepted the resignation of the short-time CEO who has led the drive for expedited approval and construction of the Antelope Valley Station to Neset Transmission Project and replaced him with a long-time Basin executive. This makes now an appropriate time to reconsider the assumptions and judgments behind the project.

To be frank: Is this project needed? Here is what Basin says.

> Within the Basin Electric service area, northwestern North Dakota is experiencing a rapid increase in development as a result of the activities associated with oil extraction from the Bakken shale formation, currently concentrated in McKenzie, Mountrail and Williams counties. The level of development that has occurred and is planned for the future will require numerous infrastructure upgrades throughout the region, including an increase in electrical transmission capacity and reliability. Studies of power supply for the region and the upper Midwest (Integrated System [IS], 2011) indicate that a new 345-kV transmission line and associated substation additions and upgrades are needed to increase the capacity to distribute electricity to serve the long-term needs of northwestern North Dakota. In addition, the project is expected to help maintain the reliability of the delivery system. The purpose of this analysis is to identify an acceptable route that minimizes the impacts on the environment and regional socioeconomic resources of the AVS to Neset Transmission Project.

Screen capture from Basin Electric, Supplemental Draft EIS, December 2013

And here is the source cited for the need statement above.

> IS (Integrated System). 2011. Eastern Montana/Western North Dakota Load Serving Study facility Additions Justification-August 2011.

Screen capture of citation for paragraph immediately above

IS, Integrated System, is an entity that goes back to a 1962 agreement binding together Basin Electric and the Western Area Power Administration to build and maintain power transmission lines—another creature of public entrepreneurship. Thus the authority cited for the need to build the current transmission line is an entity dedicated to the building of transmission lines.

Throughout the hearings on the Basin proposal convened first by the North Dakota Public Service Commission and then by the Rural Utilities Service, there has been a notable paucity of representations stating need for the transmission line. Examining rosters and statements, it seems that those testifying to such need are Basin executives, residents of communities where Basin operates power plants, landowners who stand to benefit financially from Basin's purchase of easements, and cooperatives who are long-term clients of Basin.

One of them testified on January 16 that "members who may want additional electricity or new members wanting electricity at a new home site, water well or commercial location will eventually be refused service for the sake of keeping the lights on for those who are currently being served"—as quoted in a news release from Basin. Note the use of passive voice. The statement is not that the region will have to go without power. Rather, the fear is that Basin will not be the company to supply the power.

Given the acute situation described by Basin and its clients, we would expect a public outcry from communities and consumers desperate for power. We still await that outcry (which may well be manufactured, now that its lack has been noted).

Viewed historically, the Antelope Valley Station to Neset Transmission Project appears to be an attempt by a traditional lignite-based power supplier located in central North Dakota, using the advantages of federal funding, to preempt market share in the growth region of northwest North Dakota, thereby suppressing the growth of local generating capacity that would use abundant natural gas, obviate the need for Basin's transmission line, and establish long-term economic improvement in the northwest.

Northwest North Dakota is the global epicenter of available, unexploited, going-to-waste natural gas, an excellent basis for power generation. The idea that the lights will go out unless Basin Electric is allowed to build its transmission line across North Dakota's most significant historic site is preposterous. It is a case of carrying coals to Newcastle.

Indeed, the problems with the Basin Electric arguments are so large, and so glaring, they are visible from outer space.

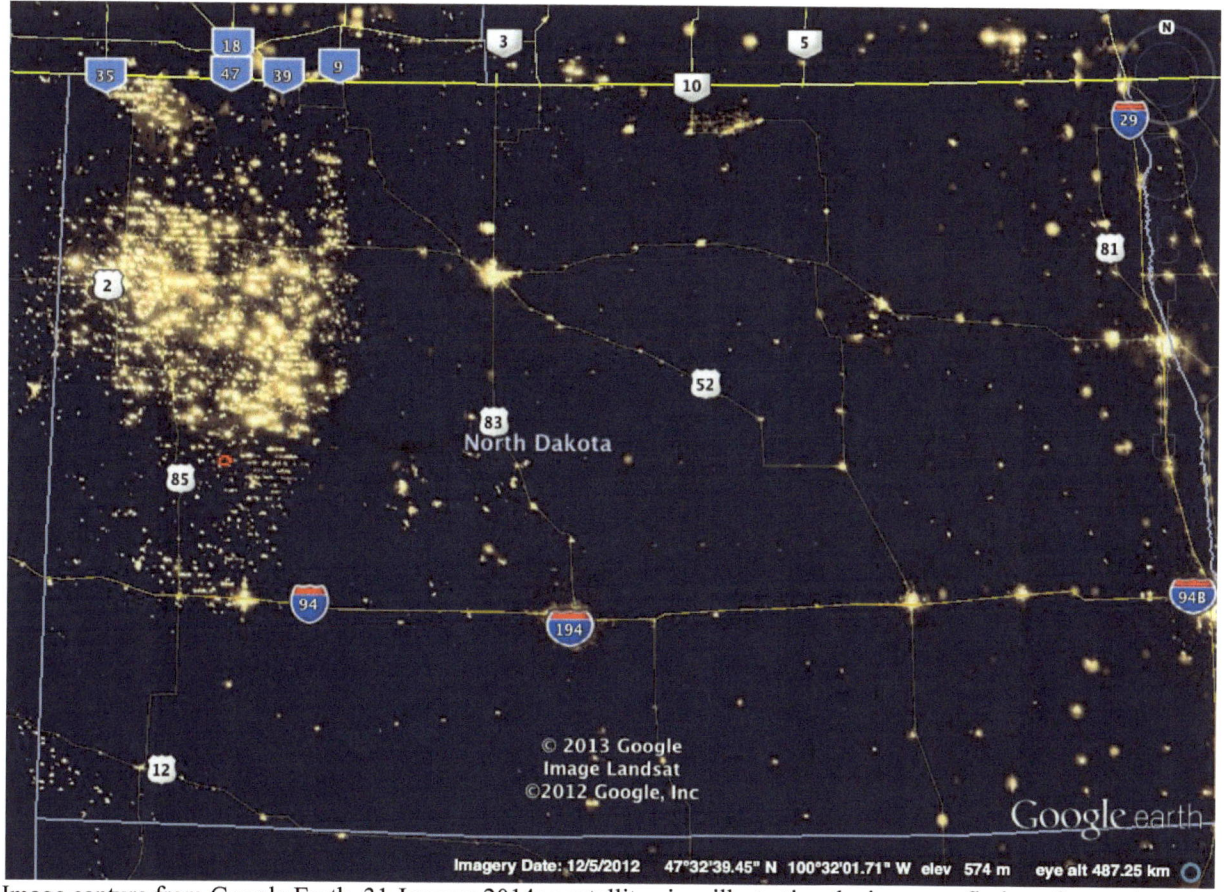

Image capture from Google Earth, 31 January 2014: a satellite view illustrating the immense flaring of natural gas in the Bakken production region, where Basin Electric proposes to remedy the shortage of energy with a 365kV transmission line across the Killdeer Mountain Battlefield (battlefield marked by red dot)

Alternatives

Multiple parties, including the Killdeer Mountain Alliance, have pointed out the failure of Basin Electric to offer alternative sitings for its 365kV transmission line. None has yet pointed out the obvious flaw in the logic of Basin's proposal and refusal to offer alternatives. Basin argues that it is vitally necessary it be allowed to build a transmission line into northwest North Dakota. It professes to be gravely concerned about the people of this prospective service region. In that case, would not a well-managed firm, concerned with the public interest, be worried about the vulnerability of a proposal posing only one alternative? What if the single alternative proved to pose a prohibitive problem—such as the degradation of the state's most significant historic site, or perhaps some matter of public safety heretofore undetected? It simply beggars belief that intelligent management would go down this dangerous road.

Is there an explanation for this apparently foolhardy course? To investigate, we turn to a document provided the Public Service Commission by Basin Electric in October 2011: *Macro-Corridor and Alternatives Report for the AVS to Neset 345-kV Transmission Project*. This document explains the decision process for choosing a macro-corridor (5 miles wide) for a transmission line and for choosing a specific route within a corridor. The document is explicit about the criteria used.

On page 5.7 the study explains a key opportunity for siting a transmission line.

5.3.3 Transmission Lines

Existing transmission lines may provide opportunities for routing the proposed transmission line adjacent to an existing right-of-way. Paralleling the rights-of-way of existing transmission lines could potentially reduce environmental impacts associated with construction, operation, and maintenance of the proposed transmission line and is considered good routing practice by confining linear facilities to common corridors. However, it is not practicable for this Project to parallel existing high-voltage transmission lines (above 230-kV) for reasons of system reliability unless where multiple lines greater than 230-kV merge at common points such as the AVS and Charlie Creek substations. For the Project, Basin has indicated opportunities for placing the proposed transmission line adjacent to an existing line are limited to within 0.50 mile of existing 230-kV or lower voltage transmission lines to preserve system reliability.

Existing transmission lines within the macro-corridors are shown in Figure 5-7. Large areas within the macro-corridors are void of any high-voltage transmission lines, although distribution lines are found throughout the macro-corridors. There are two Basin Electric 345-kV transmission lines extending from the AVS Substation in the extreme eastern part of macro-corridor segment A. A Western 115-kV line, which is to be upgraded in 2012 to 230-kV, enters macro-corridor segments B and D south of Williston and generally parallels U.S. Highway 85 to the south until terminating at the existing Charlie Creek 345-kV Substation. An MDU 115-kV and Basin Electric 230-kV line extend from the existing Williston 230-kV Substation through a portion of macro-corridor segment F before connecting at the existing Neset 230-kV Substation. These lines provide some opportunities to be paralleled by the proposed project, but they do not extend in the direction necessary for this project for long distances.

We are concerned here not about "long distances," but rather with a segment of a transmission line near and across the Killdeer Mountain Battlefield. Basin's 2011 submission clearly states, "Existing transmission lines may provide opportunities for routing the proposed transmission line adjacent to an existing right-of-way" in order to "potentially reduce environmental impacts associated with construction, operation, and maintenance." More broadly, "this is considered good routing practice." Concerns of "system reliability," it is noted, might make it "not practicable . . . to parallel existing high-voltage transmission lines (above 230-kV)." Note, precisely, the definition of "high-voltage transmission lines" that might preclude co-location of another transmission line: such lines would be "above 230-kV." The consideration, then, is crystalline: if there is an existing right-of-way, and the existing transmission line is not above 230kV, then the use of the existing right-of-way is not precluded. In fact, its use is to be considered "good routing practice."

Is there such an existing right-of-way in the locality of the Killdeer Mountain Battlefield, which might be used in order to avoid degradation of the historical integrity of the battlefield? The answer, according to Basin's submission, is yes, categorically and graphically.

See the map on the page following, reproduced from Basin's document. Closely paralleling Highway 200, running to the south of the battlefield, is an existing right-of-way. It is color-coded blue, which color denotes "Existing 115-kV & 230-kV Transmission Lines." Thus this line is not "above 230-kV." Basin's own study says that to use this right-of-way would be "good routing practice."

This is truly perplexing. Basin offers no explanation as to why it chose to ignore "good routing practice" and instead designate a route through the middle of the Killdeer Mountain Battlefield. (There have been secondhand reports that Basin representatives have expressed qualms about the security of building alongside an existing transmission line, but these have surfaced only after public advocates of battlefield preservation have raised the issue, not during the planning process, and no one has explained away the clear mandate in Basin's own study to pursue "good routing practice.")

The only explanation that seems feasible and logical is that Basin may be holding this preferable route in its back-pocket, as a backup or future alternative. This leaves us wondering what else we are not being told. We have only examined only one, obvious alternative. Surely assiduous research would produce others.

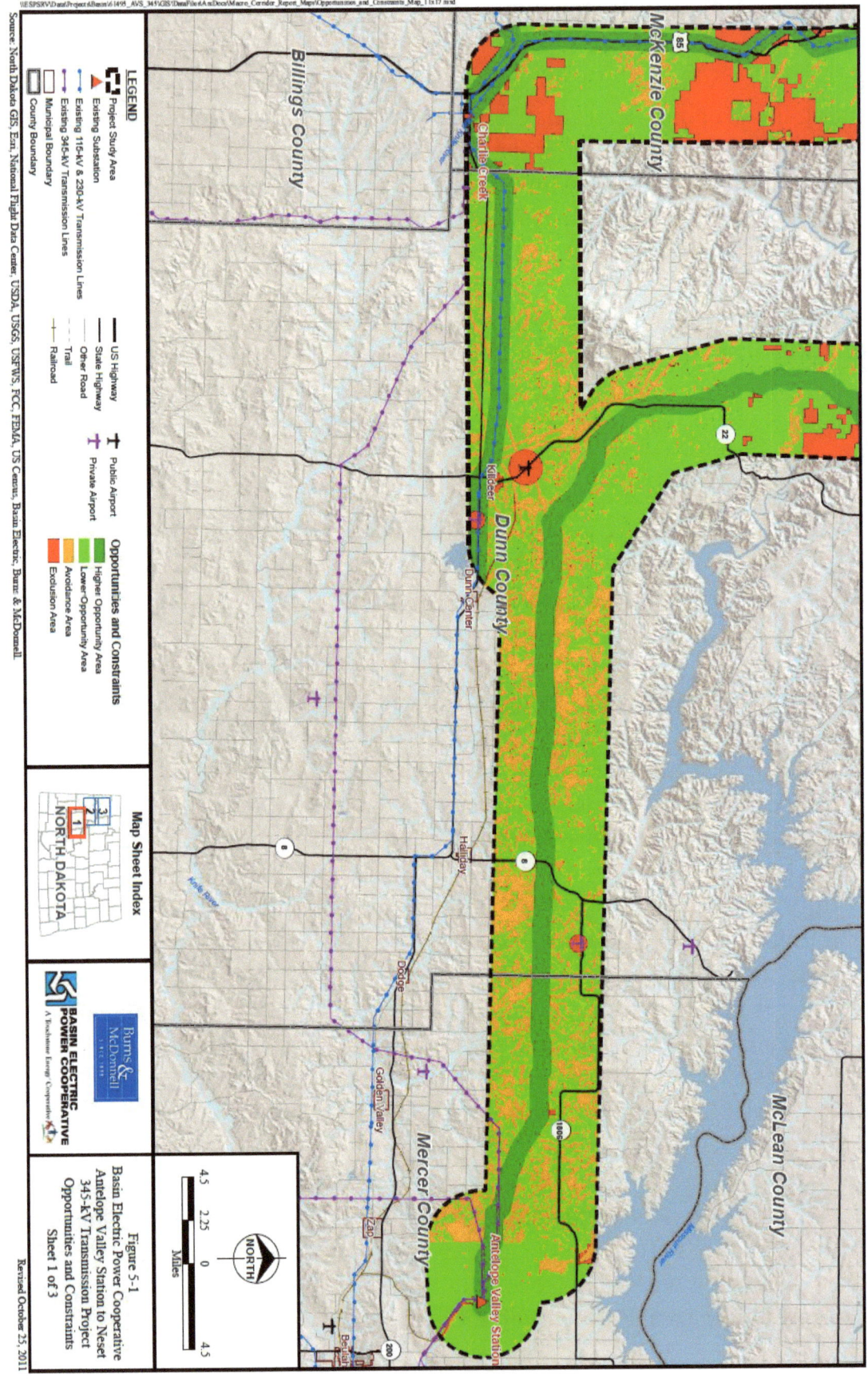

Figure 5-1
Basin Electric Power Cooperative
Antelope Valley Station to Neset
345-kV Transmission Project
Opportunities and Constraints
Sheet 1 of 3

Cover-Up

In the submission by the Center for Heritage Renewal to the Public Service Commission on September 4, 2013, the center pointed out the obvious flaws in the cultural resource studies and draft environmental impact statement done to that point. The cultural resource studies were (and remain) incomplete; the portions submitted failed in multiple aspects to meet the stipulations of the State Historical Society of North Dakota for such studies; they were based on inadequate and ineffectual research. Most seriously, they failed utterly to identify and evaluate the most important site in the project area, the Killdeer Mountain Battlefield, despite abundant documentation, including the work of the National Park Service, readily available online. This resulted in the inclusion of false statements in the DEIS, including the categorical (and categorically false) verdict, "No adverse effects on NRHP [National Register of Historic Places] eligible cultural resources."

At the time, although highly critical of this shoddy work, we were inclined to chalk it up to inattention and error. Subsequent disclosures, however, make this diagnosis no longer tenable. Evidence indicates that knowledge of the Killdeer Mountain Battlefield, knowledge of its historical significance, and knowledge of its spatial extent were in possession of the parties to the process, and such knowledge was suppressed, resulting in false statements included in the EIS given for consideration by the PSC.

A common tool used by historians in order to discern relationships and potential relationships among historical events is the simple timeline. Therefore, at this point we insert a timeline of events pertaining to the Basin Electric proposal for the Antelope Valley Station to Neset Transmission Project, up to the date when the center submitted to the PSC.

14 December 2009	State Historical Society of North Dakota announces $1.3 m. contribution from Touchstone Electric Cooperatives	Basin Electric most prominent donor in the presentation
June 2010	National Park Service issues (and posts to web) its update to Civil War battlefields in North Dakota	Information on sites provided by SHSND; NPS says of all such sites, "Killdeer Mountain is most at-risk"
5 December 2011	BE files letter of intent	First filing in Case PU-11-696

	with PSC	
Date unknown	State Historic Preservation Office receives Level 1 cultural resources survey on project	[Unable to obtain this report]
7 February 2013	SB 2341 Hearing Government & Veterans Affairs Committee ND State Senate	ND SHPO testifies as to cultural significance Killdeer Mountain and in favor of a $250,000 appropriation to SHSND for its survey
		Following otherwise wholly positive testimony by multiple parties and interests, landowner Brian Dvirnak denounces the bill as dangerous government intervention, effectively killing the bill
		Also present: Kimball Banks, Metcalf Archeology; Merl Paaverud, SHSND; Tim Reed, SHSND
15 March 2013	BE files with PSC for waiver of procedures & timelines	Request includes stipulation of a narrow, 150'-wide corridor
April 2013	SHPO receives *preliminary* Level 2-3 cultural resource survey on project	Report notes that fieldwork is not complete; states there are no historic sites of concern
13 July 2013	News of grant by American Battlefield Protection Program to Center for Heritage Renewal, to study Killdeer Mountain Battlefield, appears in state press	News released to press before NDSU is notified of grant
23 July 2013	BE files amendment to its request for waiver	Stated criteria for avoidance: "Designated or registered national: historic districts; wildlife areas; wild, scenic or recreational rivers; wildlife refuges; and grasslands," as well as "Historical resources which are not specifically designated as exclusion or avoidance areas"
		Documentation <u>four times</u> declares categorically, "No adverse effects on NRHP eligible cultural resources."
23 August 2013	Letter by Susan Veigel Dickey to	First press notice of BE intent to build transmission line across Killdeer Mountain

	Dunn County Herald	Battlefield
29 August 2013	News article by Lauren Donovan in *Bismarck Tribune*	First statewide notice of BE intent to build transmission line across Killdeer Mountain Battlefield
3 September 2013	CHR requests from SHSND information as to status of cultural resource survey filed by MA	[No reply ever received]
3 September 2013	SHSND letter to PCS re mitigation plans	Letter states that SHSND "received and initially commented on" the April preliminary report by MA [have been unable to obtain comments]
4 September 2013	PSC hearing on PU-11-696 in Killdeer	Aaron Barth presents submission by CHR; Craig Dvirnak declares (in writing) his support for BE construction; multiple parties, native and white, protest Basin plan to degrade the Killdeer Mountain Battlefield

The chronology begins with a regrettable circumstance: the prominent role of Basin Electric in philanthropic giving to the State Historical Society of North Dakota, at least since 2009.

We emphasize that there is no direct evidence that donations by Basin Electric or associations to which it adheres have affected administrative and regulatory decisions made by the State Historic Preservation Office of the SHSND. We make no such allegation. We simply note that it is regrettable, and a sign of systemic flaws in heritage administration, that at the time the SHSND has been exercising administrative and regulatory authority over high-profile projects advanced by Basin Electric, the SHSND has been in a visible position of receiving financial support from Basic Electric.

The consequence is a public perception damaging to the credibility of the regulatory process. The SHSND should have the opportunity to dispel the untoward images of recent associations.

Unfortunately, public perception of such associations is unlikely to improve, as public proceedings continue to highlight the giving of Touchstone Energy, and most prominently Basin Electric, to the State Historical Society of North Dakota.

North Dakota Heritage Center
Major Donors Give $3.1 Million for Expansion Project

Volume 40, Number 4 - Winter 2009

By Rick Collin

Two major donors' gifts this winter have brought the expansion project of the North Dakota Heritage Center nearly to the point where groundbreaking for construction can occur this summer. The 2009 Legislative Assembly authorized $51.7 million for the expansion of the exhibits and collections spaces of the state museum. Of this, $39.7 million in state funds was appropriated. An additional $12 million must come from private and federal funds, with at least $6 million of this pledged before construction can begin.

The State Historical Society of North Dakota (SHSND) Foundation has raised $5.6 million in private donations to date.

Donors and supporters pose after a December 14 news conference announcing the Touchstone Energy Cooperatives' donation of $1.3 million for the expansion of the North Dakota Heritage Center. (l to r) Jon McMillan, president, SHSND Foundation Board; Marlo Sveen, SHSND Foundation development director; Virginia Nelsen, SHSND Foundation executive director; Wally Beyer, SHSND Foundation Board vice president; Ron Harper, general manager and CEO of Basin Electric Power Cooperative; Al Christianson, manager of business development and North Dakota governmental affairs for Great River Energy; Dennis Hill, vice president and general manager of North Dakota's Association of Rural Electric Cooperatives; and Governor John Hoeven. Oklahoma-based Continental Resources, Inc. has donated $1.8 million for the expansion project. At right, chairman and CEO Harold Hamm speaks at a luncheon following the January 22 news conference. Joining Hamm in making the announcement were Governor Hoeven and U.S. Senator Byron Dorgan (D-ND).

Plains Talk (SHSND newsletter)

Tesoro, USDA Forest Service Fund Updated *Passport, History on Call* Program

By Andrea Winkjer Collin

A third edition of the award-winning *Passport to North Dakota History*, a traveler's guide to historic sites, has been republished for this summer's tourist season with a $25,000 donation from Tesoro. The theme for this year's passport is the *Power of the Past – the Journey Begins Here*.

This edition highlights the significance of the energy sector to the history of North Dakota. Two new partners, the North Dakota Department of Transportation and Basin Electric Power Cooperative, donated services to develop a fold-out map, which shows the locations of all historic attractions featured in the guide, as well as more than 40 communities with Tesoro locations. On the flip side of the map

> is the North Dakota Energy Trail, featuring more than 20 stations, mines, wind farms, and other energy sites, many offering tours, with interesting facts and histories of those facilities.

Plains Talk Fall 2010

> **2014 Recognition Event Planned:** On April 24, 2014, the Foundation will host its second Recognition and Thank You Event honoring Touchstone Energy Cooperatives, Inc. for their $1.3 million donation to the expansion of the North Dakota Heritage Center. The theme for the event will be "the power of human connections." Touchstone members are Basin Electric Power Cooperative, North Dakota Association of Rural Electric Cooperatives, Great River Energy, Minnkota Power Cooperative, Inc., and National Information Solutions Cooperative. Other honorees will be A Kirk and Janet Lanterman, Tesoro, and USDA US Forest Service, the late Governor William Guy and the North Dakota Legislature. The event will be held at the Ramkota Hotel. Everyone is welcome. Contact the Foundation office for advance ticket sales.

Plains Talk Winter 2014

An important benchmark in the timeline is the June 2010 release of the National Park Service document, *Update to the Civil War Sites Advisory Commission Report on the Nation's Civil War Battlefields: State of North Dakota*. This document has been continuously available via the internet; it shows up in any rudimentary web search. The color cover photo of the document is an image of Killdeer Mountain. It places Killdeer Mountain on the map of North Dakota and maps the areal extent of the Battle of Killdeer Mountain. It notes, "Each of North Dakota's battlefields remains a good candidate for comprehensive preservation, but **Killdeer Mountain** is most at-risk."

Proponents of the Basin project have alleged that the NPS document is not reliable because it lacks on-the-ground verification. Here is the NPS statement on research methods.

> ### Research and Field Surveys
> The ABPP conducted the field assessments of North Dakota battlefields in August and September of 2008. The surveys entailed additional historical research, on-the-ground documentation and assessment of site conditions, identification of impending threats to each site, and site mapping. Surveyors used a Global Positioning System (GPS) receiver to map historic features of each battlefield and used a Geographic Information System (GIS) program to draw site boundaries. The ABPP retains all final survey materials. Each battlefield survey file includes a survey form (field notes, list of defining features, list of documentary sources, and a photo log), photographs, spatial coordinates of significant features, and boundaries described on USGS topographic maps. The surveys did not include archeological investigations for reasons of time and expense.

The NPS also solicited information and expertise from the State Historical Society of North Dakota. Here is its acknowledgment of "respondents."

> **Respondents** Keith Giesler, Whitestone Hill Battlefield Historical Society; Diane Rogness, State Historical Society of North Dakota; Paul Van Ningen, U.S. Fish and Wildlife Service, Long Lake Wetland Management District; and Jeb R. Williams, North Dakota Game and Fish Department

Curiously, the SHSND, despite its own participation in the NPS study, did not update its site files using the information provided to and by the NPS. Nevertheless, the sound grounding and ready availability of the 2010 NPS study gives the lie to any statement in cultural resource practice that the significance and extent of the Killdeer Mountain Battlefield was somehow unknown.

Basin Electric first came before the Public Service Commission with a filing in December 2011. Shortly thereafter its hired cultural resource firm, Metcalf Archeology (Kimball Banks, regional manager and principal investigator for North Dakota), commenced the cultural resource studies that the Center for Heritage Renewal has criticized as deficient. Such studies are submitted to the SHPO at the SHSND and are required to meet professional standards published on the SHSND website. There was little or no public notice of heritage matters associated with the Basin proposal for more than a year.

Late in 2012 petroleum development in the Killdeer Mountain locality prompted public concern with heritage conservation in the region (although there still was no public notice of the Basin proposal in this regard). Consequently, a group of state senators brought Senate Bill 2341 into the 2013 legislative session. The bill, which ultimately did not pass, proposed an appropriation of $250,000 to the State Historical Society of North Dakota to do a study of the Killdeer Mountain Battlefield. The Senate Government & Veterans Affairs Committee took testimony on the bill on February 7, 2013.

By this time the Center for Heritage Renewal already had made application to the American Battlefield Protection Program of the National Park Service for a grant to study the battlefield. That application was pending. It had been duly submitted to and approved by North Dakota's designated state official for intergovernmental compliance, under a process dating back to the Reagan administration by which state agency proposals to federal programs must be reviewed to ensure that they are in congruence with state programs and policies. The center, despite the pending status of the proposal, had distributed public information on the application to the

ABPP. Fern Swenson and Merl Paaverud of the SHSND testified in favor of the bill, as did Tom Isern of the center in support of the SHSND. At the hearing on February 7, there was discussion before the committee as to how a prospective study by the SHSND might interface with a prospective study by the center. Also present and testifying (against the bill) was Brian Dvirnak, who therefore heard the entire discussion (a pertinent fact, inasmuch as Dvirnak, in representations to other landowners and to the public, subsequently would claim to have been uninformed about the matter).

The photograph below, taken at the state senate hearing on February 7, 2013, depicts participants and attendees.

Dakota Goodhouse, an enrolled Standing Rock Sioux, is speaking. To his left (with hat) is Isern, preparing to testify, and conferring with Paaverud. To his left is Swenson, and to her left, Tim Reed, also of ND SHPO.

Of particular interest is the person seated at lower left and wearing a black puffer jacket. This is Kimball Banks, Metcalf Archeology, who at this time was principal investigator in charge of cultural resource survey work on the Basin transmission line project.

Unknown to center staff and the other people in the room (Dvirnak, SHSND staff, and Banks excepted), while this hearing was going on, Basin Electric was formulating its proposal to build a 365kV transmission line across the very site of concern, and Metcalf Archelogy was providing the cultural resource studies in support of the project.

Lest there be any doubt as to the situation of this photograph, at right is an enlargement (difficult to read in this printing, but clearly indicating date and bill) of the whiteboard that appears therein.

Let there be no doubt: Metcalf Archeology and ND SHPO were fully aware of the significance and location of the Battle of Milldeer Mountain throughout the formative stages of Basin Electric proposals and Metcalf Archeology studies. For reasons unknown, the facts were omitted from the studies, which were nevertheless accepted by ND SHPO.

Following the legislative attention of early 2013, Basin Electric accelerated its review process, going to the PSC in March to request waiver of procedures and timelines. It is to be noted that despite the failure of the state senate bill, the center was now publicly known to have applied to the ABPP for a grant to study the Killdeer Mountain Battlefield, and the center had a track record of success with this NPS program. Curiously, Metcalf Archeology chose in April 2013 to submit a "preliminary" report of cultural resource findings, an unusual practice. These circumstances indicate a quickening of Basin resolve on the transmission line project during the time when the ABPP was considering the center's grant proposal.

On July 13, 2013, the *Fargo Forum* published a brief news note stating that the ABPP had awarded a grant to the center for the Killdeer Mountain Battlefield study. The center had not yet been informed of the ABPP decision, and it would be months before contracts would be signed at both ends. Still, precisely ten days after the *Forum* notice, Basin again came before the PSC to amend its request for waiver of procedures, stating no less than four times, "No adverse effects on NRHP eligible cultural resources."

There can be no doubt that these were false statements. There is no proof, however, that Basin personnel were aware the statements were false. It is possible that their cultural resource contractors shielded them from the knowledge of the significance and location of the Killdeer Mountain Battlefield.

To this time, then, there was no public notice, and certainly no knowledge on the part of center staff, that Basin Electric was planning to build a transmission line across the Killdeer Mountain Battlefield. That information so far had been successfully covered up. The knowledge was forthcoming when a letter to the editor of the *Dunn County Herald*, published on August 23, 2013, revealed the threat to the historic site. Reading of this in coverage by the *Bismarck Tribune*, center staff, observant of their state-approved mission, decided to make a submission to the PSC hearing in Killdeer on September 4. The center was unaware Basin Electric had been busy signing easements with landowners, including owners of the Killdeer Mountain Battlefield, for power line construction. Financial terms of such agreements are not released to the public.

In more recent months, Basin representatives repeatedly have declared that they could not have known there was a problem with building a transmission line where they proposed, because no one protested. Could this be because public knowledge of the line's route across the Killdeer Mountain Battlefield, the Gettysburg of the Plains, had been so effectively suppressed?

Diversions

Two days before the hearing, Isern sent the center's full submission to the PSC by email. On September 4 Aaron Barth, assistant director of the center, traveled to Killdeer to present the submission before the PSC. What happened next was surprising.

Essentially, Barth had come to Killdeer to provide the PSC the cultural resource information that Basin Electric and its contractors had failed to provide. This might have been regarded by the PSC as a service, but instead Barth was hectored. After Basin representatives were allocated abundant time for exposition, Barth attempted to present the center submission. The presiding judge cut him off after only a brief time, and questioning by PSC members began. A member of the PSC from the locality in which Basin Electric operates its power generation facilities, Randy

Christmann, questioned Barth aggressively, demanding to know why the center had submitted a proposal to study the Battle of Killdeer Mountain without first obtaining permission of all landowners, rather than only some landowners.

The germane fact in regard to this exchange is that the center submission did not deal with, or even mention, the ABPP-funded study, which had not yet begun. Nor does that study, scheduled to last two years, have anything to do with consideration of the Basin proposal; chronologically, it cannot. Nevertheless, the proceedings of the hearing, which might have explored the significance of the historic site and raised alternatives in order to preserve it, were hijacked in order to criticize the center for even contemplating a study that, in fact, had nothing to do with the stated purpose of the hearing.

Landowner Craig Dvirnak attended the hearing in Killdeer and took the opportunity to score Barth and the center for proposing to study the battlefield. He also, alongside his signature on the hearing attendance sheet, avowed his support for the Basin proposal.

Hearing Attendance Sheet

Case Number PU-11-696   Date Sept 4, 2013

Name	Address	Phone	Testifying? Yes/No
Aaron Barth	PO Box 5097, Fargo 58105 North Dakota State University, Center for Heritage Renewal	701-425-7342	Yes; Against
Don Hedger	P.O. Box 655 Killdeer, ND	701-764-5467	
Patrick Hedger	1038 2nd ST. SW Killdeer	701-764-5634	
Senator Heidi Heitkamp Rep.	Dickinson	701 225-0974	Gather info
MARK NYGARD	MAYOR - HAZEN ND	701 891 9748	SUPPORT
Craig DVIRNAK	Killdeer, ND	1-701-863-6730	Support

For six weeks thereafter, the center submission to the PSC was not published on the PSC website, although submissions by other parties who had not even attended hearings were published. The center submission was published only after center staff made personal appeal to Commissioner Brian Kalk.

(Along similar lines, it might be noted that on November 4, 2013, the center mailed copies of its PSC submission to Rod O'Sullivan, NEPA Document Manager,

Antelope Valley Station to Neset Transmission Project EIS, Western Area Power Administration, and to Dennis Rankin, Project Manager, Engineering and Environmental Staff, Rural Utilities Service, with copies to Senator John Hoeven, Senator Heidi Heitkamp, and Congressman Dennis Kramer—see Appendix 3. None of these agencies or parties has acknowledged receipt of the material.)

Following the center submission in Killdeer, interested parties commenced a concerted diversionary attack on the center and its proposed battlefield study, thereby avoiding discussion of the degradation of the battlefield implicit in the Basin proposal. Craig and Rhonda Dvirnak, landowners, claiming to speak for multiple landowners, engaged an attorney to warn the center that access to private lands in the battlefield area would not be forthcoming, and distributed a letter to that effect widely. Dvirnak also wrote the president of North Dakota State University and the chancellor of the North Dakota University System to defame the director of the center and to attempt to suppress research on the battlefield. The campaign descended into personally abusive communications directed at the center director, of which the email reproduced below is a sample.

Tom Isern <isern@plainsfolk.com>   9/17/13

to Bryan

Greetings, Bryan! Good to hear from you. Please feel free to call me at 701-799-2942, day or night. I look forward to talking with you.

Tom Isern
Professor of History & University Distinguished Professor
Director, Center for Heritage Renewal

NDSU NORTH DAKOTA STATE UNIVERSITY

On Mon, Sep 16, 2013 at 8:20 PM, Bryan Dvirnak <bdvirnak.cci@midconetwork.com> wrote:
> Tom, you've just of been had! Stay tuned. You tried to pull a quick one in the 2013 Legislature and now again with the National Park Service. You lied to my brother Craig Dvirnak about the research grant. You may be intelligent, but you are stupid and your behavior supports my statement.

With landowners fronting the diversionary campaign, Basin Electric began shopping the landowner grievances to editorial boards of major daily newspapers, sometimes succeeding in procuring buy-in for their stated grievances. At the same time, Basin representatives, in public statements, presented the controversy over the battlefield degradation as an unfair criticism, expressed too late, having to do with a theoretical designation of the battlefield area—ignoring the most definitive statements extant, those of the National Park Service.

The public relations campaign assumed a certain genius of concerted elements: deny the significance and integrity of the battlefield, say the results are inconclusive, and at the same time, deny access to persons prepared to investigate and confirm details. ND SHPO refused to allow parties outside the Basin-Metcalf alliance to update the site form for Killdeer Mountain Battlefield, despite abundant information available to justify the update, on the grounds that there needed to be more on-the-ground reconnaissance—thus rejecting the work done by the NPS. Of course, additional on-the-ground reconnaissance was impossible, because access was denied. Thus concerted firewalling succeeded in preventing any other parties from bringing new information to bear on the issues at hand.

All the while, landowners who had signed agreements with Basin Electric to build a 365kV transmission line across the most significant historic site in North Dakota kept proclaiming that they were the best custodians of the site's heritage.

What bearing does this sad story of information suppression and public disinformation have on the matter before the Rural Utilities Service, which decides whether taxpayer money should be spent to build Basin's transmission line? The point is that the RUS is receiving its information base from individuals, organizations, and processes that have proven themselves, at best, unreliable.

Impacts

Given the unreliability of intelligence previously provided by Basin Electric and its clients, it seems almost futile to comment on the most recent update of the DEIS, filed by Basin with the PSC January 8, 2014. Here, however, are some brief comments.

Section 3.6 is devoted to "Cultural Resources." There are debilitating problems with this section, including demonstrably false statements.

For instance, the document alleges at the outset,

> During the September 2013 NDPSC administrative hearing on Basin Electric's Route Permit Application for the proposed project alignment, several entities expressed concerns about the possible direct and indirect impacts of project construction on the Killdeer Mountain Battlefield.

> The DEIS recognizes the relationship between the project and the 1-acre Killdeer Mountain Battlefield State Historic Site. However, the DEIS does not acknowledge a more extensive boundary for this battlefield because that information was not on file at the State Historical Society of North Dakota, and neither the agencies nor the public provided comment on the potential impact of the project on the Killdeer Mountain Battlefield.

As demonstrated above, the information was "not on file" because the SHSND chose not to put it into the site file. The SHSND had the information, in fact provided the information to the National Park Service, and was fully aware of the National Park Service designation of the battlefield. Metcalf Archeology also was fully aware of this information, and moreover, was specifically obligated, under its charge from the SHSND, to bring it forward parcel to the cultural resource survey process, but declined to do so. The DEIS raises a false distinction by saying the absence of specific site file information about the Killdeer Mountain Battlefield justifies excluding it from consideration. That statement deliberately ignores the SHSND's explicit instructions to contractors to go beyond mere site files, which often are minimalist, and to use every information source available. Basin and Metcalf failed to do what they were required to do. They now claim that their failure to do their research somehow excuses them from taking into account the integrity of the battlefield.

There is another, even more explicit, problem with the passage above, as the DIES claims, "neither the agencies nor the public [making representations at hearings] provided comment on the potential impact of the project on the Killdeer Mountain Battlefield." This, we regret to say, must be adjudged a deliberate falsehood. The Center for Heritage Renewal made both oral and written submission to the PSC, and we provided explicit comment on the impact of the Basin project on the battlefield (see Appendix 1). We applied the stated guidelines of the National Park Service (the agency which houses the National Register of Historic Places, the source of all evaluative criteria for significance and integrity of historic sites) as to integrity of historic battlefields, showing that whereas many modifications of land use are acceptable without destruction of integrity, the building of a 365kV transmission line across the middle of a battlefield is exactly the type of change most destructive of integrity. The new DIES has failed to answer this. Instead, it denies, falsely, that such guidance exists.

Later in the cultural resources section, the DIES addresses the question of definition of the battlefield and misrepresents the National Park Service study released in 2010. The DIES says, "NPS acknowledged that the study and core area boundaries, as proposed in the 2010study, had not yet been field-verified or confirmed through archeological or historical examination." In fact, as recounted above, the NPS said no such thing. The NPS said it based its findings on its own fieldwork and on information provided by the SHSND. The statement to the contrary is unsupported by any evidence that the NPS misrepresented its work, and thus appears to be another instance of attempting to discredit the authority of the NPS because its findings are inconvenient.

In the next paragraph the DIES attempts to discredit the legitimacy of the battle site by belittling it as merely a "site lead" and quoting SHPO verbiage to the effect that a site lead comes from a "nonprofessional." Are we to take from this that NPS staff are "nonprofessional"? The more damning circumstance is that the only reason the battlefield has only a "site lead" and not a "site file" at the SHSND is that ND SHPO stubbornly refuses to allow a site file for the battlefield to be created, despite abundant basis for it. That refusal, coupled with deployment of the "site lead" argument based on it, is disturbing.

In the subsequent discussion of impacts, the DIES submission concedes the significance of the Killdeer Mountain Battlefield and accepts the NPS maps as the basis of working boundaries. It goes on to argue, however, that petroleum and attendant developments in the locality "have significantly compromised the battlefield landscape and its viewshed." The DIES continues to ignore more specific guidelines provided by the NPS in 2010 and instead falls back on the more general criterion for integrity, "whether or not a participant in the battle would recognize it as it exists today."

This, of course, sounds like a judgment call. It is the professional judgment of the Center for Heritage Renewal that the battlefield most certainly retains sufficient integrity for National Register designation. The DIES seems to agree, but emphasizes that there are other industrial intrusions in the landscape, which make a 365kV transmission line, an unprecedented intrusion on the site, seem not so bad. The DIES provides an unsophisticated and impressionistic discussion of visual impacts of the proposed transmission line that places a 365kV transmission line in the same category of disturbance as a three-wire barbed wire fence.

Conclusions

The sections in this submission make the following major points.

1. There is a lack of credible evidence for the need of Basin Electric to build the Antelope Valley to Neset Transmission Project, and strong evidence it is unneeded.

2. Basin has failed to explain why it has rejected other, superior line sitings and instead proposed only one, which runs across the middle of the most significant historic site in North Dakota.

3. Vital information as to the significance and location of the Killdeer Mountain Battlefield has been suppressed and withheld from regulatory authorities.

4. A concerted campaign of disinformation has sought to divert public and agency attention away from the deliberate degradation of the Killdeer Mountain Battlefield implicit in the Basin proposal.

5. The Basin proposal entails unacceptable and unnecessary degradation of the integrity of the Killdeer Mountain Battlefield as a historic site.

It is possible to back up from the myriad documents and tangled processes that have brought us to contemplate an unprecedented degradation of our state's most significant historic site. Since 1971 economists have been aware of a powerful undertow known as "regulatory capture," as described by University of Chicago economist George J. Stigler ("The Theory of Economic Regulation," *Bell Journal of Economics and Management Science* 2 [Spring 1971]: 3-21). Stigler's concept of regulatory capture is well-known; indeed, it is a staple of conservative thought in modern America.

Stigler posits that although the public generally thinks regulatory agencies exist for public benefit, "regulation is acquired by the industry and is designed and operated primarily for its benefits. . . . The most obvious contribution that a group may seek of the government is a direct subsidy of money." Surely Stigler's argument resonates through the expectation by Basin Electric of taxpayer support for its construction of a transmission line. "When an industry receives a grant of power from the state," Stigler continues, "the benefit to the industry will fall short of the damage to the rest of the community." In the case of Basin's proposed transmission line, the damage falls most directly on a heritage resource: the Killdeer Mountain Battlefield.

In proposing its transmission line, Basin Electric was permitted to hire and direct its own consultant for survey and evaluation of heritage resources: Metcalf Archeology. Metcalf worked for Basin and was paid by Basin. Metcalf is dependent on contracts from Basin and other industrial clients. It can hardly be surprising that its reports, published SHSND guidelines to the contrary, failed to note such an evident but inconvenient fact on the ground as the Killdeer Mountain Battlefield. The flawed cultural resource reports led to a flawed DEIS, containing false assertions, submitted to the PSC. We might expect that ND SHPO, a function of the SHSND, possessing its own regulatory authority, might compel honesty and professionalism in such submissions, but our expectation is tempered by knowledge of the dependency of the SHSND on financial support from Basin and its allied cooperatives. Right through to the current DIES update, the same consortium of allied interests continues to churn out flawed statements. In the meantime, when a party external to the process, the Center for Heritage Renewal, charged by the state to provide expertise in heritage conservation, attempted to insert information not bought and paid for by Basin, it was chided by the state regulatory authority and subjected to a campaign of defamation and intimidation by industrial interests.

The jury is still out as to whether the Rural Utilities Service, too, is captured, but so far, the evidence is not good. The Killdeer Mountain Alliance (see Appendix 4) has pointed out the deficiencies in scheduling and public notice for the RUS hearing convened in Watford City on January 16, 2014. (That hearing went ahead despite bad weather and dangerous road conditions. A group of dedicated citizens attended, nevertheless, driving the most dangerous roads in North Dakota through the bad weather, in order to voice their protests of the regulatory capture evident in Basin's progression through the regulatory process.) The experience of the center is that the RUS is no better than other agencies about even acknowledging receipt of information critical of Basin's proposal.

The strong evidence of regulatory capture here described indicates a need for fundamental reconsideration of processes. Indeed, PSC member Julie Fedorchak spoke in these terms at the PSC hearing in Killdeer on September 4, 2013. In the meantime, however, we have the matter at hand: a proposal to build a 365kV transmission line across the Killdeer Mountain Battlefield.

This submission by the Center for Heritage Renewal to the Rural Utilities Service makes strong statements about the failure of processes and about the actions of agencies and individuals. They are sufficient, we contend, for simple denial of project support. It would be better, however, for the ongoing effectiveness of process, to get to the bottom of the disputes here treated. If Basin Electric, or any other parties, believes they have been misrepresented, then let them all have the opportunity to explain everything. Under oath.

We therefore suggest that the Basin Electric proposal be sent back to the North Dakota Public Service Commission for additional consideration and public hearings. The PSC has the power to compel testimony under oath. Let us see what the process looks like in the light of day.

Submission to North Dakota Public Service Commission

By the Center for Heritage Renewal
North Dakota State University

Director: Tom Isern, Professor of History
& University Distinguished Professor
Assistant Director: Aaron Barth

Subject: Killdeer Mountain Battlefield
RE: Case # PU-11-696

Abstract

The Killdeer Mountain Battlefield, where Dakota and Lakota fighters fought the Northwest Expedition of Brigadier General Alfred Sully, is an exceedingly significant historic site worthy of preservation and respect. Unfortunately, proposals here under review call for a power transmission line to be built across the core of the battlefield. This is an unacceptable denigration of the integrity of the site. Further, the study documents on which the proposals are based are unacceptably deficient. The Center for Heritage Renewal applauds the heroic efforts of Basin Electric to build the infrastructure of development and life in western North Dakota. Its concern is with the heedless and needless destruction of heritage resources of incalculable value, specifically the historic site of the Battle of Killdeer Mountain, 28 July 1864—the Gettysburg of the Plains.

Center for Heritage Renewal

The center was established by State Board of Higher Education on 17 May 2006. Its authorized mission is "to identify, preserve, and capitalize on the heritage resources of North Dakota and the northern plains." The center is charged both "to assist state agencies, private organizations, and the people of the state and region in generating prosperity and quality of life from heritage resources" and also to provide "expertise and action in the fields of historic preservation and heritage tourism." Because of its express mission and objectives, the Center for Heritage Renewal provides this submission to the Public Service Commission.

Center for Heritage Renewal - Tom Isern, Director
isern@plainsfolk.com / 701-799-2942

Battle of Killdeer Mountain

The Battle of Killdeer Mountain, also known as the Battle of Tahkahokuty, was the climactic engagement of the Dakota War in Dakota Territory.

During the summer of 1864 there commenced the gathering of native peoples at Tahkahokuty, a traditional encampment for the season, but one assuming military significance at this juncture of the Dakota War. Based on previous experience fighting columns of white soldiers, native strategists considered Tahkahokuty the best position for a confrontation with invading forces. First arrived Lakota elements, specifically Hunkapapas, including the young leaders Gall and Sitting Bull. Additional Lakota arrived: Sans Arc, Miniconjous, and Blackfeet. They all were moved to resistance by the trespass on their lands of white gold miners bound for Montana. Next came a large complement of Yanktonais, aggrieved over the assault by Sully on their encampment at Whitestone Hill the previous year. Finally, there was a group of Santee, largely Mdewakanton and Wahpekute Dakota, led by Inkpaduta, who had more experience fighting the whites than anyone else. Sully at one point estimated the number of fighters emplaced to confront him at Killdeer Mountain at 6000. More likely it was closer to 2000, with much larger numbers of noncombatants.

It might be asked, why were thousands of lodges of noncombatants in camp on Tahkahokuty, where the native strategists intended to fight? The answer is, General Sully was waging total war against them, the purpose being to crush them as a people, through destruction of their material goods and assaults on women and children. The Dakota and Lakota wished to fight Sully at Killdeer Mountain, and only the presence of their encampment would bring the enemy there to fight. Clearly, the native strategists expected to defeat Sully's army on this favorable ground.

After consolidating his forces at Fort Rice on the Missouri River, Sully and his Northwest Expedition of 1864 moved west to engage. Leaving some troops in camp on the Heart River, he led a strike force northwest to where his scouts told him the Indians awaited him. Sully's force comprised some 2200 men, augmented by scouts, mainly Yankton and Winnebago. His best troops were Brackett's Battalion of Minnesota Cavalry, men seasoned by eastern campaigns of the Civil War, remounted and issued new carbines, revolvers, and sabers for the expedition. Also with him were elements of the 6th Iowa Cavalry, the 7th Iowa Cavalry, the 1st

Dakota Cavalry, the 8th Minnesota Infantry, the 2nd Minnesota Cavalry, and two batteries of artillery comprising eight pieces, mainly 12-pound mountain howitzers.

It is important to establish who the combatants were, since these are the people who fought and died at Killdeer Mountain. The action that took place there on 28 July 1864 is well recounted in works listed in the bibliography—those of Clodfelter and Beck are standard accounts, with that of Beck the better. The best single narrative of the engagement, because it recognizes Indian agency and strategy, is provided by NDSU student Sara Sjursen and derives from a research seminar in spring 2013.

Sully divided his troops into two brigades and formed them into a phalanx, or square, to advance upon the native position on the slopes, his cavalry advancing dismounted, but re-mounting to counter native offensive moves. Dakota and Lakota fighters arrayed themselves in assault groups and attempted to break up the soldiers' formation, but were countered by effective use of artillery. The evident hope was to use the coulees and canyons of the mountain to advantage in order to stop the soldiers in their ascent toward the encampment, then engage in close fighting. Timed fuses on artillery shells made it possible, however, to hit native forces taking cover in the broken terrain. Nevertheless, the two sides were fighting to what amounted to a spectacular draw when Sully's forces raised the stakes of the battle: they turned the artillery on the women and children gathered on the mountain to observe the fighting. This caused the majority of the losses suffered that day and compelled precipitous retreat by the Indians. They evaded pursuit by evacuating northwest into the Badlands. The soldiers destroyed the encampment and the food and material left there. There were atrocities committed in the camp, including the killing of captured children by the Winnebago scouts.

The Battle of Killdeer Mountain was a defeat for the Dakota and Lakota. Although the Dakota elements thereafter were not able to muster effective resistance, the Lakota remained assertive and were not cowed. Soon after they would confront Sully's army again in the Battle of the Badlands, a touch-and-go engagement which the troops were fortunate to survive.

Due to reliance on artillery, soldier casualties at Killdeer Mountain were light, only five deaths, including two pickets killed as Sully withdrew from the scene of action. Indian casualties exceeded 100, likely were closer to the estimate of 150 given by Sully, and included a majority of noncombatants.

The areal extent of the Battle of Killdeer Mountain has been mapped by the National Park Service in its 2010 report on battlefields in North Dakota. Although many peripheral moves are yet to be situated with certainty, it is known that the main combat action took place rather precisely where submissions by Basin Electric plot a 345-kV power transmission line.

Significance of the Battle

The points of historical significance associated with the Battle of Killdeer Mountain are many and cumulative, in sum making the Killdeer Mountain Battlefield the single most historic site in North Dakota. In the interest of conciseness, we list major points of significance here as numbered items.

1. This was the largest single military engagement ever to take place on the Great Plains of North America. It was a rare event for there to be massed forces on both sides in Indian-white conflict on the plains. No other single engagement matches Killdeer Mountain for fighters engaged on the two sides.

2. Killdeer Mountain was the place chosen by Dakota and Lakota leaders to confront the Northwest Expedition of Brigadier General Alfred Sully. Because it offered tactical advantages, this place was strategic ground. It was no accident the battle happened here.

3. The Battle of Killdeer Mountain was pivotal in the destruction of Dakota sovereignty on the northern plains and in the reshuffling of Dakota peoples into new aggregations based on defined reservations (Sisseton-Wahpeton, Standing Rock, Spirit Lake). Notwithstanding continuation of scattered hostilities, Killdeer Mountain brought concerted armed resistance by Dakota peoples to an end.

4. The Battle of Killdeer Mountain brought Lakota peoples to the fore in hostilities resisting white occupation of the northern plains. Within two weeks of the engagement, Lakota fighters would assault Sully's army again in the Battle of the Badlands. Their fight for their country would continue until the late 1870s, sequencing through what are commonly referred to as Red Cloud's War of the mid-1860s and the Sioux War of the mid-1870s.

5. The Killdeer Mountain Battlefield is a place of somber remembrance. Here United States soldiers fought and died. Here, too, more tellingly, Dakota and

Lakota defenders of their homeland fought and died, along with large numbers of noncombatants. This is a place of heroism and of tragic sacrifice.

Deficiencies of Process

It seems sensible to ask how we have arrived at the point where an expertly managed and socially responsible firm such as Basin Electric is asking to build an intrusive power transmission line across the middle of the most historic site in North Dakota, a place properly considered a site of somber remembrance in honor of our dead, native and white. Once again we resort to numbered points for the sake of conciseness and clarity.

1. The cultural resource section of the environmental impact statement submitted to the Public Service Commission is grievously flawed. It is based on a preliminary report submitted to the State Historical Society of North Dakota by a consulting archeology firm. This report (SHPO reference 12-1016) purports to be a Level II and Level III survey of cultural resources in the project area. In fact, it does not even meet the minimal requirements for a Level I survey, because it lacks the required review of literature that guidelines say should precede and guide field survey work. Its bibliography is less than one page. (We include in our submission a three-page selected, preliminary bibliography of sources on the Battle of Killdeer Mountain, to show how much good source material was missed.) Because of the failure to conduct the literature search, the consultants omitted the Battle of Killdeer Mountain from their list of cultural resources in the project area. (The one-acre state historic site at the battlefield gets a mention, but not the battlefield itself.) No researcher went so far as to consult a county history, or even to conduct a Google search—which would have surfaced the National Park Service's 2010 report on Civil War sites in North Dakota, with its color cover photo depicting Killdeer Mountain. These omissions of method and content in the preparation of information for submission to the SHSND and the PSC are unacceptable.

2. Indeed, the lack of a proper review of literature, which is intended to guide fieldwork, makes the whole survey suspect. Researchers entered the field unprepared for the material culture they might encounter and uninformed as to known historic sites.

3. The cultural resources report is mainly devoted to surface archeology, but its bibliography contains no works specific to the known resources of the region, such as Knife River Flint, to choose an obvious example.

4. The historical resources inventoried are mainly sites of agricultural settlement, but the bibliography contains no sources dealing with agricultural settlement or its material culture. Nor is there any evidence that historians were involved in evaluating historic resources.

5. Neither the cultural resource survey nor the environmental impact statement makes any mention of tribal consultations. People of the Sisseton-Wahpeton, Standing Rock, and Devils Lake reservations were directly involved with the Battle of Killdeer Mountain. Even if there has been some unrecorded contact with tribal historic preservation officers, certainly no one has told them of the intent to build a transmission line through the middle of the Killdeer Mountain Battlefield, because project studies have failed to note its existence. Other native peoples of the region, too, regard Killdeer Mountain as holding deep cultural significance. We do not presume to speak for them. We only note that they must be asked to speak to this issue.

6. Finally, the cultural resource survey on file with the SHSND is labeled "preliminary." Thus project managers have come to the PSC for approval without having completed their homework.

In sum, the processes for survey and inventory of cultural resources have failed—they failed to locate the most salient heritage resource in the project area, and are deficient in other ways—and cannot be accepted as reliable by the PSC or any other authority.

Impacts of Basin Electric Proposal

Cultural resource survey work on the project emphasizes surface archeology and only evaluates direct, physical damage that might be done to specific artifactual material. This completely misses the point in regard to a historic site such as Killdeer Mountain. The significance of the site is established and unquestionable. What the proposed project imperils is its integrity. Here is what the National Park Service says on the subject of battlefield integrity.

> Significant changes in land use since the Civil War do diminish the integrity of the battlefield landscape. Heavy residential, commercial, and industrial development; cellular tower and wind turbine installation; and large highway construction are common examples of such changes. Battlefield landscapes

with these types of changes are generally considered as having little or no integrity.

In light of this statement, there can be little doubt that construction of a 345-kV power transmission line across the middle of the Killdeer Mountain Battlefield will leave it with "little or no integrity."

This, too, falls short of stating the fundamental issue at stake. The Killdeer Mountain Battlefield is a site of remembrance, of heroism and tragedy, where our citizens, Indian and white, must be able to reflect upon our common heritage. A 345-kV power transmission line across the middle of this hallowed ground is disruptive and disrespectful. As North Dakotans, we must be better than this.

Conclusion

Given the facts and circumstances stated above, we feel confident that Basin Electric, the people of North Dakota, and their Public Service Commission will do the right thing. Indeed, let this unfortunate episode be a lesson to us, and an occasion for respectful remembrance as we approach the 150th anniversary of the Battle of Killdeer Mountain, the Gettysburg of the Plains.

We would be remiss in our charge from the state board and in our responsibilities as public servants not to point out that the placing of this matter before the Public Service Commission at this time and in this form is cause for reflection and recalibration. The case exposes systemic flaws and fundamental deficiencies in our policies and procedures for heritage conservation, flaws and deficiencies that might go unnoticed for years or decades, but that become acutely obvious during a time of intense resource and infrastructural development. The Center for Heritage Renewal welcomes any opportunity to examine and remedy these flaws and deficiencies, which do not serve development well, and which place our heritage resources in peril. As responsible North Dakotans, we must, going forward, do better. Here and now, as practical North Dakotans, we need to solve this problem of a power transmission line proposed to run through the heart of the Killdeer Mountain Battlefield, indeed, through the heart of our heritage.

Selected Bibliography on the Battle of Killdeer Mountain

Ackermann, Gertrude W. "George Northrup, Frontier Scout," *Minnesota History* 19 (1938): 377-392.

Andrews, C. C., Ed. *Minnesota in the Civil and Indian Wars, 1861-1865*. St. Paul: Pioneer Press, for State of Minnesota, 1890.

Bean, Geraldine. "General Alfred Sully and the Northwest Indian Expedition," *North Dakota History* 33 (Summer 1966): 240-59.

Beck, Paul N. *Columns of Vengeance: Soldiers, Sioux, and the Punitive Expeditions, 1863-1864*. Norman: University of Oklahoma Press, 2013.

Beck, Paul N. *Inkpaduta: Dakota Leader*. Norman: University of Oklahoma Press, 2008.

Bergemann, Kurt D. *Brackett's Battalion: Minnesota Cavalry in the Civil War and Dakota*. St. Paul: Borealis Books, 2004.

Brackett, Alfred B. Alfred B. Brackett Papers, 1861-1868. Minnesota Historical Society, St. Paul.

Brackett's Battalion and Fifth Iowa Infantry Minutes. 1915. State Historical Society of North Dakota, Bismarck.

Campbell, Sylvester Starling. Diary. State Historical Society of North Dakota, Bismarck.

Chaky, Doreen. *Terrible Justice: Sioux Chiefs and U.S. Soldiers on the Upper Missouri, 1854-1868*. Norman: Arthur H. Clark, 2012.

Clodfelter, Michael. *The Dakota War: The United States Army Versus the Sioux, 1862-1865*. Jefferson: McFarland & Co., 1998.

Dauntless Dunn. Dunn Center: Dunn County Historical Society, 1970 (Vol. 1) & 1989 (Vol. 2).

Drips, J. R. "Three Years Among the Indians." Carbon copy, State Historical Society of North Dakota, Bismarck.

Froebel, Charles. "Notes of Some Observations Made in Dakota, during Two Expeditions, under Command of General Alfred Sully, in the years 1864 and 1865." Offprint of article, no citation, NDSU Archives.

"Further Details of Gen. Sully's Battle with the Sioux," *New York Times*, 18 October 1863, reprinted from the *Winona Republican*.

"History of General Sully's Indian Expedition--It Returns to Sioux City," *St. Joseph Herald & Tribune*, reprinted by *Daily Alta California*, 14 January 1865.

"Iowa Troops in the Sully Campaigns," *Iowa Journal of History & Politics* 20 (1922): 364-443.

Jenkins, David N. David N. Jenkins Papers, 1864, 1904-13. Minnesota Historical Society, St. Paul.

Jones, Robert Huhn, *The Civil War in the Northwest: Nebraska, Wisconsin, Iowa, Minnesota, and the Dakotas*. Norman: University of Oklahoma Press, 1960.

Kelly, Fanny. *Narrative of My Captivity among the Sioux Indians*. Cincinnati: Wilstach, Baldwin & Co., 1871.

Kiederback, A. A., et al. *Report of the Killdeer Mountain Park Commission, 1919*. North Dakota: The Commission, 1919.

Kingsbury, D. L. Map of Minnesota: Showing Route of the Northwestern Indian Expedition of 1864. State Historical Society of North Dakota, Bismarck.

Kingsbury, David Lansing. "Sully's Expedition against the Sioux in 1894," *Collections of the Minnesota Historical Society* 8 (1898): 449-62.

McConnell, Richard. Diary. State Historical Society of North Dakota, Bismarck.

Myers, Frank. Diary. State Historical Society of North Dakota, Bismarck.

Myers, Frank. "Facing the Reds: Indian Fighting under Sully in the Northwest," *National Tribune*, 6 August 1896, 13 August 1896, 20 August 1896, 27 August 1896.

Neely, Mortimer. Abstract of the History of Captain A. B. Brackett's 3rd Company, Minnesota Cavalry. Minnesota Historical Society, St. Paul.

Orland, Ole N. Ole N. Orland Papers. State Historical Society of North Dakota, Bismarck.

Pfaller, Louis. *Sully's Expedition of 1864, Featuring the Killdeer Mountain and Badlands Battles*. Bismarck: State Historical Society of North Dakota, 1964.

Robinson, Elwyn B. *History of North Dakota*. Lincoln: University of Nebraska Press, 1966.

Seeger, William. "Sully's Sioux Campaign: Journal of a Member of Brackett's Battalion, Minnesota Cavalry," *National Tribune*, 5 October 1899, 12 October 1899, 19 October 1899, 26 October 1899, 2 November 1899, 9 November 1899, 16 November 1899, 23 November 1899.

Sjursen, Sarah. "The Battle of Killdeer Mountain," paper presented to the Senior Seminar in History, North Dakota State University, Spring 2013.

Stoddard, J. S. Map Showing the Route Traveled by the Sully Expedition, 1864. Minnesota Historical Society, St. Paul.

Sully, Langson. *No Tears for the General: The Life of Alfred Sully, 1821-1879*. Palo Alto: American West Publishing Company, 1974.

United States. Department of the Interior. National Park Sedrvice. American Battlefield Protection Program. Update to the Civil War Sites Advisory Commission Report on the Nation's Civil War Battlefields: State of North Dakota. Washington, 2010. http://www.nps.gov/hps/abpp/cwsii/CWSACReportNorthDakotaUpdate.pdf.

United States. War Department. *The War of the Rebellion: A Compilation of the Official Records of the Union and Confederate Armies*. 4 series, 70 vols. Washington: Government Printing Office, 1880-1901.

Utley, Robert M. *The Lance and the Shield: The Life and Times of Sitting Bull*. New York: Ballantine, 1994.

Wells, Willoughby. "Brackett's Battalion of Minnesota Cavalry Company B," Genealogical Records Committee, Daughters of the American Revolution for the State of Minnesota, Box 6, Volume 35, 1945, 121-27.

Appendix 2
Cover art of 2010 NPS study depicting Killdeer Mountain Battlefield

Center for Heritage Renewal

PO Box 1390 / Fargo ND 58107-1390
heritage.renewal@gmail.com

4 November 2013

Rod O'Sullivan, NEPA Document Manager
Antelope Valley Station to Neset Transmission Project EIS
Western Area Power Administration
P.O. Box 281213
Lakewood, CO 80228-8213

Dennis Rankin, Project Manager
Engineering and Environmental Staff
Rural Utilities Service, Utilities Program
1400 Independence Avenue SW., Mail Stop 1571
Washington, D.C. 20250-1571

Dear Mr. O'Sullivan & Mr. Rankin:

Enclosed here is a copy of a submission made by the Center for Heritage Renewal to the North Dakota Public Service Commission in the matter of PSC Case PU-11-696, which is on your books as the Antelope Valley Station to Neset Transmission Project, as proposed by Basin Electric Power Cooperative. The document is posted by the PSC here –

    http://www.psc.nd.gov/database/documents/11-0696/069-010.pdf

I take the liberty of sending this inasmuch as the document was not immediately posted by the PSC, and so my intent is to make sure the submission does not escape notice. The submission contains important information about the draft EIS in your possession and posted at your website—specifically, that the EIS is based on a grievously flawed cultural resource study, one that neither satisfies rudimentary state requirements for such a study nor is complete.

The result of the failure to conduct stipulated survey and review functions in regard to cultural resources is that the EIS contains incorrect information, such as the categorically false statement, "No adverse effects on NRHP eligible cultural resources." The submission here enclosed demonstrates that the transmission

Cont.

Isern to O'Sullivan & Rankin cont.

line project promises catastrophic effects on the most significant historic site in North Dakota, the Killdeer Mountain Battlefield—a site not only NRHP eligible but also profoundly significant to American history.

Copies of this submission are going also to US Senator Hoeven, US Senator Heitkamp, and US Congressman Cramer, inasmuch as the Basin Electric proposal entails the expenditure of significant federal funding in the destruction of this historic site in North Dakota.

The Center for Heritage Renewal, an applied-research center of North Dakota State University, is charged by the state to identify and preserve its heritage resources, not only as a legacy to posterity but also as a palpable resource. The submission here enclosed was prepared expressly in pursuit of this state mandate.

Regards,

Tom Isern, Director
Center for Heritage Renewal
North Dakota State University

cc: US Senator John Hoeven
338 Russell Senate Office Bldg.
Washington DC, 20510

US Senator Heidi Heitkamp
SH-502 Hart Senate Office Building
Washington, DC 20510

US Congressman Kevin Cramer
1032 Longworth House Office Building
Washington, DC 20515

**Statement of Rob Sand
on behalf of the Killdeer Mountain Alliance
regarding the December 2013 Supplemental DEIS for the Basin Electric Power Cooperative's (Basin Electric) Antelope Valley Station
(AVS) to Neset Transmission Project
January 16, 2014, Watford City, ND**

Thank you for the opportunity to make a statement at this public hearing concerning this important project. I am speaking on behalf of The Killdeer Mountain Alliance, a group of individuals working to preserve the cultural, spiritual, ecological, archaeological, and historical integrity of the Killdeer Mountains.

We learned of this meeting as a result of a press release dated January 10, 2014 published by Basin Electric and made available on the internet. Apparently the Rural Utility Service limited its notifications to other media as no other information regarding the meeting is available on the internet, which we as a scattered membership must rely upon for timely information.

Yesterday we learned that a Federal Register Notice was published by the Rural Utilities Service on Tuesday, January 14, just two days ago regarding this project. It states: "RUS will hold an open-house public hearing in January 2014 once the SDEIS is published. The time and location of the meeting will be well advertised in local media outlets a minimum of 15 days prior to the time of the meeting." This commitment was not met; the notice of this meeting appeared in the Dunn County Herald on January 10, just six days ago. ~~This edition of the Herald has not yet even been received by its mail subscribers.~~ The January 14th Federal Register notice further states: "Public Participation: Pursuant to 36 CFR 800.22(d)(3), it is the intent of RUS to use its NEPA procedures for public involvement in lieu of the public involvement requirements of 36 CFR 800.3 through 800.7." If you pursue this reference, you will find it does not exist; apparently the Rural Utilities Service intended to refer to CFR 800.**2**(d)(3) which authorizes the use of agency procedures for public involvement under the National Environmental Policy Act.

The rush to hold this meeting is more than contemptuousness of the public input element of the NEPA process, it is reflective of the haste and superficiality of the investigations and analysis of alternatives that support this project in general and the Supplemental Draft Environmental Impact Statement (SDEIS) in particular.

The SDEIS for the Antelope Valley Station to Neset Transmission Project was developed to expand the alternatives considered because the original ones would not meet the current demand projections for movement of electrical energy in Western North Dakota. Equally important from our perspective was that for the first time the Rural Utility Service and the other cooperating agencies more appropriately recognized the extent and significance of the Killdeer Mountain Battlefield as an important element of America's Civil War experience. It is truly an important historical and cultural site from the perspective of both the Union Army forces and the Native Americans who fought and died there.

The fundamental problem with the SDEIS is that it develops no alternative that would avoid constructing eight miles (that is right, eight miles) of transmission lines though the heart of the Killdeer Mountain Battlefield. Consequently it fails to comply with the requirements of the National Environmental Policy Act (NEPA).

Section 1502.1 of the Council on Environmental Quality's NEPA implementing regulations states: "The primary purpose of an environmental impact statement is to serve as an action-forcing device to insure that the policies and goals defined in the Act are infused into the ongoing programs and actions of the federal government. **It shall provide full and fair discussion of significant environmental impacts and shall inform decisionmakers and the public of the reasonable alternatives which would avoid or minimize adverse impacts or enhance the quality of the human environment."**

Section 1502.14 of The Council on Environmental Quality's regulations further requires agencies to: **"Rigorously explore and objectively evaluate all reasonable alternatives, and for alternatives which were eliminated from detailed study, briefly discuss the reasons for their having been eliminated."** The National Park Service recognizes the Killdeer Mountain Battlefield as a place eligible to be placed on the National Registry of Historic Places. Proceeding to degrade a noteworthy historic site without even analyzing alternatives which would avoid doing so is unconscionable and fails to comply with the requirements of NEPA and the Council on Environmental Quality's Implementing Regulations (40 CFR Parts 1500-1508).

It must be kept in mind that the reason that an Environmental Impact Statement is being prepared is because Basin Electric is requesting Federal taxpayer subsidies for constructing the transmission project. As concerned citizens, we find it to be absurd that one agency of the Federal government, in this case the Department of Agriculture's Rural Utility Service, would even consider using its funds to degrade the Killdeer Mountain Battlefield. After all, its sister Federal agency, the National Park Service of the Department of the Interior, used taxpayer money to study and to identify the battlefield site as a place worthy of protection through its inclusion on the National Register of Historic Places.

What must be done to avoid degrading this unique historical and cultural site on the 150th anniversary of the Battle of Killdeer Mountain, which took place on July 28, 1864? The project must be sent back to the drawing board. Alternatives that avoid crossing the battlefield must be evaluated in a detail comparable to analysis of the present alternatives. It must be demonstrated that it is not practicable to avoid degrading the Battlefield site. Only then will the requirements of the Environmental Protection Act be satisfied, and we as citizens and taxpayers can have confidence that the decisions of government are indeed in the public interest.

www.ingramcontent.com/pod-product-compliance
Lightning Source LLC
Chambersburg PA
CBHW042130040426
42450CB00003B/139